LANCASHIRE

A Glossary of the Lankyshire Dialect

ABSON BOOKS LONDON

5 Sidney Square London E1 2EY England

Dedicated to the memory of Jack Lowe -
a real Lancashire lad

ABSON BOOKS LONDON

5 Sidney Square London E1 2EY England

First published in Great Britain, November 1997
7th impression August 2007

Compiled and edited by Fred Holcroft
© Fred Holcroft
Cover design by Chris Bird

From a photograph by kind permission of Scalpay Linen

Printed by Gutenberg Press, Malta
ISBN 978 0 902920 97 2

PREFACE

The Lankyshire dialect encompasses several different sub-dialects which peacefully co-exist between the River Mersey and the sands of Lune. To the north of the region Lakeland and Northumbrian influences predominate, while to the South the posh people of Cheshire speak Standard English while their social inferiors are almost Midlanders in dialect. At one time or another Lancashire has been home to Celts, Romans, Saxons, Vikings and Normans, all of whom have left their stamp on the language, even if the accent does change from St. Helens through Wigan and Bolton to Preston, Burnley, Oldham, Rochdale and Manchester. Although the Scousers of Liverpool are historically and geographically part of Lancashire, they have evolved an accent, dialect, culture, an entire way of life even, all of their own.

The nineteenth century, together with the early years of the twentieth, was the golden age of the Lankyshire dialect. Books in dialect abounded, notably by Ben Brierley, John Collier (aka Tim Bobbin), Sam Fitton, Sam Laycock, Edwin Waugh, and Ammon Wrigley. Where some regional dialects have only survived in a rural atmosphere the Lankyshire dialect thrived during the industrialisation of the county. In fact the industries themselves were a rich source of new dialect words.

The Lankyshire dialect survived almost untouched until after the Second World War, as can be seen from the 1930s and 1940s films of George Formby, Gracie Fields and Frank Randle, but first the eleven-plus, then the comprehensive system, and finally the gentrification of the working classes dealt it a series of body blows.

Yet the dialect lives on, kept alive not only by the grit of the people but by the efforts of the Lancashire Dialect Society, which caters for the ordinary dialect speaker as well as those with a more exalted academic interest in spoken language.

Here are over 450 words and phrases to help you understand the Lankyshire dialect, together with a guide to pronunciation which shows how it is spoken.

Fred Holcroft

A

aback	behind (*"aback on 'im"*)
abaht	about
abee	alone
abide	to tolerate, to stand (*"ah caunt abide 'im"*)
acre	field, regardless of size
afeart	frightened
afore	earlier, before
agate	(1) start; (2) against (*"gerr agate quick ees agate on us"*)
ah	I
aht	out
ail	ill

akint	same as
ale can	alcoholic
alley	marble
allus	always
anall	also
apiece	each
appen	perhaps
arto?	are you?
as	(1) who; (2) has ("*'im as as the pub next door*")
aside	beside
ast?	have?
asto?	have you?
awbut	nearly
awlreet	correct
awlrung	incorrect
aye	yes
az	(1) has; (2) I've ("*az ee bin? az no idea*")

B

backeend	(1) Autumn; (2) last few days of the week
backert	backwards
backs	narrow passageway between buildings (see also 'entry' and 'ginnel')
baggin	packed lunch, usually taken to work (see also 'jackbit' and 'snap')
bally	stomach
banister	rails on stair and landing
bant	(1) strength; (2) twine
barm cake	bread roll
bat	(1) to strike hard; (2) bun
battin'	speeding
bee boes	sleep
beer bally	large stomach
belter	really good (see also 'blinder', 'gradely' and 'purler')
bide	to wait
billio	enthusiastic
bin	been (*"ast binmon bin?"*)

binmon	Refuse Collection Operative
blinder	really good (see also 'belter', 'gradely' and 'purler')
boggart	ghost
bossy	orders others about
bot	without
bot just	to succeed by a narrow margin
bottomin'	Spring cleaning
bowt	(1) purchased; (2) to have nothing (*"Ahve bowt nowt un ahm bowt out"*)
brast	(1) broken; (2) bored; (3) impecunious
brastin'	burning desire to relieve oneself
brat	apron
brattle	fit for work
brow	steep road
brown split	bottle of brown ale in a pint glass with a half pint of beer
butty	sandwich (fillings: 'jam-butty', 'treacle butty', 'sugar-butty', etc.)
bunged up	constipated

C

cabbagin'	to go over the mark
cadge	to borrow
called	supposed to be (*"Ees called coming"*)
cant	(1) leaning; (2) active in old age
carryin' on	extra-marital relationship (see also 'nannyin')
caunt	unable
chawve	to irritate
cheer	chair
chelp	cheek
chep	cheap
chuck	term of endearment (see also 'luv')
chunner	mutter
clack	throat
clap	to catch (*"clap owd of this"*) (see also 'cob')
clemt	hungry
clod	(1) to throw; (2) foolish person
clout	to strike hard

club	sickness benefit
club man	insurance collector
cob	to catch (see also 'clap')
cod	to fool, to tell lies
cornish	mantlepiece
corran'	mate, pal (see also 'fettler', 'marra' and 'serra'
cotter	to strike hard
crabby	lucky
crate egg	foolish person
creemt	put aside
crick	pain
croft	field
crop	haircut (see also 'pow')
crumper	really big one
cut	canal

D

dab	clever (*"ee's a dab hand at it"*)
daft	simple
dataller	labourer down the pit

degg	to sprinkle
deggin can	watering can
delve	to dig
Dicky's Meadow	trouble (*"If I don't go now I'm in Dicky's Meadow"*) (see also 'lumber' and 'pickle')
dinner	mid-day meal
dither	unable to make up one's mind
donkey stone	abrasive sandstone block used for cleaning front doorstep of terraced house (see also 'rubbing stone')
doolally	mad
duck egg	foolish person
dyke	to spy on courting couples

E

ee	he
eeard	heard
een	eyes
egg	to incite

egg wap	foolish person
eh?	what?
eht	out
eigh	a multipurpose word which can be used to attract attention (*"eigh!!"*), to question an action (*"eigh?"*), to ask a question yourself (*"eigh worrabout this?"*) or to show amazement (*"eigh!!!"*)
entry	narrow passageway between buildings (see also 'backs' and 'ginnel')
erch	pull (*"erch up thi drawers"*)
essole	ashpan under a coal fire
etn	eaten
eyt	to eat

F

faddy	fastidious with food (see also 'kysty')
fain	(1) anxious; (2) eager; (3) delighted
fairation	fair play

far	very
fast	stuck (*"ahm fast in 't'mud"*)
favvers	resembles
fawse	sly
feight	to fight
fend	to look after
fettle	(1) to mend (*"it's brokken - ahl fettle it"*); (2) condition (*"nah it's in fine fettle"*)
fettler	mate, pal (see also 'corran', 'marra' and 'serra')
fey	ugly
fit	attractive
flash	lake caused by mining subsidence
flatrib	mild beer
flit	to move house (a 'moonlight flit' is to move secretly without paying back rent)
flummoxed	confused, flustered
font	found
fot	have to (*"ahve got fot go t'work"*)

fradge	to gossip
fret	worn
frizzen	conceited girl
fur	very

G

gab	to talk nonstop
gallivant	to wander about enjoying oneself
gam	brave
gammy	injured (*"ee were gam, ee played on wi' a gammy leg"*)
ganzie	woolly jumper, pullover
gather	festering sore
gawp	to stare
geet	got, have to (*"ahve geet go t'work"*) (see also 'getten')
getten	got, have to
ginnel	narrow passageway between buildings, scene of many a lost virginity (see also 'backs' and 'entry')

giss	give me
glasses	spectacles
gley	squint (see also 'glide')
glide	squint
gob	(1) mouth; (2) to spit (see also 'golly')
gobbin	foolish person
gobshite	disagreeable character
gollop	to swallow quickly
golly	to spit (see also 'gob')
gorm	to acknowledge
gormless	stupid
gradely	really good (see also 'belter', 'blinder' and 'purler')

had up	appearing before the Magistrates
happen	perhaps
harpin'	to talk nonstop (*"stop harpin' abaht it"*)
hidin'	to strike hard

high time	the time has come
hissel	himself
homer	a real character
hont	hand
hud	to conceal
hutch	to slide closer (as on back row of cinema)

I

i'	in
Inglun	England
Inglunshoyer	all over England
insides	stomach
int	in the
iteaw	in two
ittle	it will

J

jackbit	packed lunch (see also 'baggin' and 'snap')
jaw	to grumble

jawms	sides of windows and doors
jerry	defective
jill	half a pint
jip	considerable pain
joey	confidence trick
juggins	foolish person

K

kaylied	drunk
kaylt	to beat (*"we kaylt um in extra time"*)
keck	tip over
kecks	trousers or knickers depending on where you are in the county (be careful)
keep	board and lodging
kelter	clutter
kench	sprain
kent	knew
kid	another member of your family, usually younger

kittlin'	a segment of an orange
knockin' on	getting older
knockin' shop	brothel
Kow Yed	someone from Westhoughton
kysty	fastidious with food (see also 'faddy')

L

lace	to strike hard (see also 'lamp')
lakin'	fooling about
lamp	to strike hard (see also 'lace')
landed	(1) achieved a lifetime's ambition; (2) gatecrashed a party
Lankylankylanky- lankyLankyshire	chanted by its devoted followers on every cricket ground where the Red Rose team plays
latch	to catch
leather	to strike hard
leef	as soon as
leet	(1) light; (2) to climb down; (3) to omit to pay a subscription due, especially in a card game (*"who's leet?"*)

lobby	entrance hall to terraced working-class house (to be 'lobbied off' is to be posh) (see also 'scouse')
Lobbygobbler	a native of Leigh as derisively described by a native of Wigan
lodge	reservoir to a mill or colliery
lone	lane
loyse	lose
lug	(1) to pull; (2) ear (*"open thi lugole"*)
lumber	trouble (see also 'Dicky's Meadow' and 'pickle')
lummock	clumsy person
lurry	truck
luv	term of endearment added to the end of a sentence even when talking to a complete stranger (see also 'chuck')

M

maiden	clothes horse
manderous	all-inclusive (*"ee took every manderous thing wi' im"*) (see also 'mortal')
mangy	bad-tempered
manky	scruffy
mard	soft, cowardly
mardy	spoiled child
marra	mate, pal (see also 'corran', 'fettler' and 'serra')
Mary Ann	behaving like an old woman
Mary Ellen	effeminate (see also 'Nancy' and 'Taytah')
maul	to interfere (*"stop maulin"*)
mault	stressed
maunt	don't, mustn't
mazy	dizzy (*"ah come mazy all over"*)
mee-maw	to pull faces (a legacy of lip-reading in noisy cotton mills)
meither	to pester (see also 'moider')

mendin'	sick but getting better
met	might (*"ah met but ah met not"*)
meyt	food, not just meat
mind	to be careful, to make sure (*"mind t'trams"* - a Jack Lowe special)
misen	me
moggy	cat (it is in Wigan - so there), but can also mean a mouse, or crawling insect
moggy off	get lost
moider	to pester (see also 'meither')
mon	person, always male
morn	tomorrow
morneet	tomorrow night
mortal	all-inclusive (see also 'manderous')
mothetten	exhausted (see also 'powfagged')
mun	must (*"tha mun! tha caunt do owt else!"*)
murps	marbles

N

nadger	penis
nag	to scold
Nancy	effeminate (see also 'Mary Ellen' and 'Taytah')
nannyin'	extra-marital relationship (see also 'carryin' on')
narked	annoyed
nast	dirt (*"in 'is pit nast"* means coming home from the mine without bathing)
nebber	flat cap
ned	need
neet	night
neets	night shift, night turn (*"ahr't on neets?"*)
nesh	soft, delicate, weak
never-never	hire purchase
noather	neither
nobbut	almost (*"ah nobbut geet theer"*)
nobby	head, usually a child's

nowt	(1) nothing; (2) bad-tempered, annoyed (*"ahve getten nowt un ahm nowt"*)
noww	no

O

o	all, and, as, of, on, with
oer	over
oerfaced	eaten enough food (see also 'stawed')
of	for (*"of a long time"*)
offside	sick, unwell
olung	all the time (*"ee were theer all olung"*)
on	of
our	a member of one's own family (*"Our Bob"*)
owd	old
owt	anything (*"asta getten owt?"*)

P

pad	path
parky	cold
peg out	to die
peg up	(1) to lift; (2) to give a helping hand
peggy	child's tooth
pen	allotment
petty	outside toilet (a useful question of a prospective bride is *"con't whitewash a petty?"*)
peyl	to strike hard
pickle	trouble (see 'Dicky's Meadow' and 'lumber')
pictures	cinema
pie-can	idiot
Pie-eater	a native of Wigan as derisively described by a native of Leigh
pingot	small field (see also 'croft')
plague	to tease
play	to take a day off work without permission

ponful	a lot
porr	to kick
pot	rubbish
pots for rags	foolish person
pow	haircut (see also 'crop')
powfagged	exhausted (see also 'mothetten')
powsy	dowdy
powyed	(1) bald; (2) recent haircut
purler	really good (see also 'belter', 'blinder' and 'gradely')

Q

queer	peculiar (never used in Lankyshire to describe those of the love that dare not speak its name; there are other words for that)
quick sticks	at once

R

raft	a lot (*"a raft of em"*)
rapscallion	rascal
rasper	a really good one (especially a fart)
rat's nest	untidy
rawm	(1) to wrestle; (2) to squirm
reemin'	foaming
reert	sat up
rick racks	castanets
riggot	furrow
road	way (*"this road up? Noww do it this road"*)
rook	heap (*"ee fell all of a rook"*)
root	to search obsessively
rops	kidneys
rubbin' rag	person of low status
rubbin' stone	abrasive sandstone used in cleaning front doorstep of terraced house (see also 'donkey stone')
runagate	idle

S

safe	sure, certain
sauce	to scold
scouse	(1) Liverpudlian; (2) stew (sometimes called 'lob'scouse' or 'lobby')
scrat	scratch, erase (*"scrat it aht"*)
scratchins	bits of batter, fish, chips, left behind in the chip shop range and kept in a side compartment for the discerning gourmet
scrawp	to scrape (*"we scrawped home wi' one point"*)
seet	(1) sight; (2) very much (*"mi seet's a seet better wi' mi glasses on"*)
seg	callous on hand caused by hard work
sen	(1) self; (2) since (see also 'sin')
serra	mate, pal (see also 'corran', 'fettler' and 'marra')
sex	(1) you put potatoes in them; (2) a carefully choreographed love ritual:-
fancyin' er	love at first sight

pickin' er up	she agrees to meet you
seein' er	those early dates
'angin' yer 'at up	welcomed at her parents' home
feet under t'table	accepted at her parents' home
cooertin'	engaged to be married
gerrin' wed	nuptials
livin' oert' brush	living together (see also 'livin' tally')
livin' tally	(see above and 'tally')
shape	to behave properly (*"shape thisen"*)
sharp	intelligent
sheed	to spill
shoon	shoes
shut	rid of
shuttance	riddance
side	to clear away (*"side t'table"*)
sin	since (see also 'sen')
sithee	(1) see you soon; (2) now look here
sithers	scissors
skenn	to squint (see also 'slance')

skrike	to cry
skutch	to scrape
slack	small pieces of coal
slance	to squint (see also 'skenn')
slate	to buy goods on account (see also 'strap', 'tap' and 'tick')
slavver	(1) spittle; (2) longing for food
slippy	quick
sloppy	careless
slopstone	rectangular sandstone kitchen sink
slorr	to slide
snap	packed lunch (see also 'baggin' and 'jackbit')
snigg	(1) eel; (2) to snatch
sogg	to strike hard
sogginwetthrew	drenched
sough	drain
spark	to provoke
speyk	to speak

spokken	spoken
spon	brand new
sprag	wedge
sputter	to stutter
stawed	eaten enough food (see also 'oerfaced')
steyl	(1) to steal; (2) a brush handle (*"brush steyl's come off"*)
stone jug	simple-minded
stotter	to stagger
strag	stray pigeon
strap	to buy goods on account (see also 'slate', 'tap' and 'tick')
stufft	very sick (*"mi nose is stufft"*)
sugar stealer	floating dandelion seed
suited	pleased
summat	something
sup	to drink

T

tackle	(1) to attempt; (2) a full set of male genitals
tan	to strike hard
tally	miner's identification disc (see also 'livin' tally')
tap	to pay for goods on account (see also 'slate', 'strap' and 'tick')
taytah	effeminate (see also 'Mary Ellen' and 'Nancy')
teem	to pour
teet	bound to (*"Ees teet t'do it"*)
tenter	guard dog
tha	you
that	so (*"Ahm that nowt ahm gooin'"*)
theer	there
their	member of someone else's family, including your own in-laws (*"their Doreen"*)
thi	your
think on	to remember
thisel	yourself
thronner	person good with his hands

thrutch	to strain, push hard
tick	to buy goods on account (see also 'slate', 'strap' and 'tap')
tickle	fiddly, awkward job
tidy	substantial
tip	(1) untidy heap (*"thi room's a tip"*); (2) coal mine spoil
toe rag	disagreeable person (see also 'toss pot')
toot	to pry
toss pot	disagreeable person (see also 'toe rag')
towel	to strike hard
traips	to move about to no purpose (*"stop traipsin' abaht"*)
tup	to butt with the forehead

U

ull	will
um	them
un	and

unall	as well
upstroke	finish
us	we, our, that, me (*"us all like us house us suits ussells un us suits um unall"*)
ussells	ourselves
ut	that
uzzit	letter 'z'

V

varneer	almost
varra	very

W

wag	to play truant
Wakes	annual summer holidays
wap	quick slap
warch	ache ('ballywarch' = stomach ache, 'yedwarch' = headache)
warm	to strike hard

weer	where
weet	(1) wet; (2) with it
welly	to strike hard (*"welly 'im"*)
welterin'	raining hard
wet lettuce	weakling
wick	(1) lively; (2) week
wilta?	will you?
without	unless
wom	home
woods	bowls (crown green, naturally)
woppa	anything large

Y

yah	yes
yed	head
yo	you
yon	(1) that; (2) there (*"yon mon yon"*)

IDIOMS

All up brew from here	More difficult from now on
Creakin' gate lasts longest	Don't listen to hypochondriacs
Feightin' dogs limp wom	He that lives by the sword dies by the sword
Face us ull stand cloggin'	Determined to see the situation through regardless of criticism
Get where water can't	No limit to his ability
His tap's stopped	Denied conjugal rights
Least room most thrutchin'	Those who have least about them boast the most
Looks like he's just fallen off a flittin'	Unkempt appearance (Flittings, especially moonlight ones, were usually carried out on a hand-cart - easy to fall off)
Muck or nettles	All or nothing
Peas above sticks	Ideas above your station

Stopped for bobbins	Unable to complete the task through lack of material
Throw your cap in	Give up
Once every Preston Guild	A rare event (Preston Guild is a festival held every 20 years)

Some idioms are based on the popular local game of Rugby League:

Give 'im t'dummy	Surprise move
Owt above t'grass	Anything allowed
Round t'blind side	Crafty move

PRONUNCIATION

Definite rules of pronunciation pervade this palatine northern dialect.

1. In spoken Lankyshire there is NO definite article. Liberally degg the sentence with the letter 't' so that it falls into the gaps between the words (*"are t'gooin' t'club t'neet?"*)

2. Always omit the letter 'h' when the written word begins with one, and always put one in front of any word beginning with a vowel, especially when making a speech. (*"Hit gives me henormous pleasure hon this hauspicious hoccasion to hopen the new 'ospital wing."*)

3. The single 'a' is short. Only half of one is allowed in order to make a contrast with the laah di daahs. Often the letter 'a' is changed to 'e' or 'o'. (*"Mek sum un tek it im. Con't understond mi mon?"*)

4. Double 'o's are really quadruples. Put in as many as time will allow. ("Loook at the booook worrrhe tooook.").

5. Always roll your 'r's (if you'll pardon the expression), especially in Preston where it has been canonised, in order to get back at the soft Southerners of the BBC who don't know that it exists. Keep an eye on this letter: it often jumps one place to the left. (*"Bassket's brasted un mi brid's flewd eht."*)

6. The letter 'L' is always used at the start of a word, so it is only fair to leave it out at the end of one. (*"Look lively you foo."*)

7. In Lankyshire the letter 'g' at the end of a word is usually ignored as superfluous to requirements. (*"Lerrin' im lakin' un not learnin' is addlin' is brain."*)

OTHER TITLES AVAILABLE

Language Glossaries

American English/English American
Australian English/English Australian
Irish English/English Irish
Gay Slang
Geordie English
Lancashire English
Prison Slang
Rhyming Cockney Slang
Scouse English
Yiddish English/English Yiddish
Scottish English/English Scottish
Yorkshire English
Home Counties English
Playground Slang
Hip Hop English
Rude Rhyming Slang
Military Slang

Literary Quiz & Puzzle Books

Jane Austen
Brontë Sisters
Charles Dickens
Gilbert & Sullivan
Thomas Hardy
Sherlock Holmes
Shakespeare

The Death of Kings (A medical history
of the Kings & Queens of England)

Abson Books London

5 Sidney Square London E1 2EY
Tel 020 7790 4737 Fax 020 7790 7346
email absonbooks@aol.com
Web: www.absonbooks.co.uk